# Cybersecurity in the Age of AI
## *Staying Safe in the Digital World*

# Table of Contents

1. Introduction . . . . . . . . . . . . . . . . . . . . . . . . . . . . . . . . . . . . . . . . . . . . . . . 1

2. Understanding Cybersecurity Basics . . . . . . . . . . . . . . . . . . . . . . . . . 2

   2.1. What is Cybersecurity? . . . . . . . . . . . . . . . . . . . . . . . . . . . . . . . . . 2

   2.2. Understanding the Threat Landscape . . . . . . . . . . . . . . . . . . . . . 3

   2.3. Cybersecurity Principles . . . . . . . . . . . . . . . . . . . . . . . . . . . . . . . 3

   2.4. Cybersecurity Technologies and Best Practices . . . . . . . . . . . . 4

   2.5. Legal and Ethical Considerations . . . . . . . . . . . . . . . . . . . . . . . 5

3. Unravelling the Concept of Artificial Intelligence . . . . . . . . . . . . . . 6

   3.1. Understanding the Basics . . . . . . . . . . . . . . . . . . . . . . . . . . . . . . 6

   3.2. AI Methods: How Is Artificial Intelligence Achieved? . . . . . . . 7

   3.3. The Evolution of Artificial Intelligence . . . . . . . . . . . . . . . . . . 8

   3.4. AI in Our Lives Today . . . . . . . . . . . . . . . . . . . . . . . . . . . . . . . . . 8

4. The Intersection of AI and Cybersecurity . . . . . . . . . . . . . . . . . . . . 10

   4.1. The New Cybersecurity Battlefield . . . . . . . . . . . . . . . . . . . . . 10

   4.2. Leveraging AI for Cyber Defense . . . . . . . . . . . . . . . . . . . . . . . 10

   4.3. AI as an Offensive Tool . . . . . . . . . . . . . . . . . . . . . . . . . . . . . . . 11

   4.4. Preparing for an AI-Augmented Cyber Future . . . . . . . . . . . . 12

5. Threat Landscape in the AI Era . . . . . . . . . . . . . . . . . . . . . . . . . . . . 13

   5.1. AI: Breeding Ground for Advanced Cyber Threats . . . . . . . . . 13

   5.2. AI Techniques as Cyber Threat Tools . . . . . . . . . . . . . . . . . . . 14

   5.3. How AI Changes the Threat Environment . . . . . . . . . . . . . . . 14

   5.4. Mitigating the Threats of AI . . . . . . . . . . . . . . . . . . . . . . . . . . . 15

6. AI-Driven Cybersecurity Solutions . . . . . . . . . . . . . . . . . . . . . . . . . 17

   6.1. The AI-Cybersecurity Integration . . . . . . . . . . . . . . . . . . . . . . 17

   6.2. Behavioral Analysis and Anomaly Detection . . . . . . . . . . . . . 17

   6.3. AI in Action: Pattern Recognition . . . . . . . . . . . . . . . . . . . . . . 18

   6.4. AI-Powered Phishing Detection . . . . . . . . . . . . . . . . . . . . . . . . 18

   6.5. Enhancing Incident Response With AI . . . . . . . . . . . . . . . . . . . 19

7. Role and Impact of Machine Learning in Cybersecurity . . . . . . . 21

   7.1. The Intersection of Machine Learning and Cybersecurity . . . 21

   7.2. Infrastructure Security and Machine Learning . . . . . . . . . . . . 22

   7.3. Fraud Detection . . . . . . . . . . . . . . . . . . . . . . . . . . . . . . . . . . . . 22

   7.4. Identifying and Countering Malware . . . . . . . . . . . . . . . . . . . 23

   7.5. Privacy Concerns and Mechanisms . . . . . . . . . . . . . . . . . . . . . 23

   7.6. Adversarial Attacks on Machine Learning Models . . . . . . . . 23

   7.7. Moving Forward: Ensuring the Safe Use of Machine
Learning in Cybersecurity . . . . . . . . . . . . . . . . . . . . . . . . . . . . 24

8. Risks and Vulnerabilities of AI in Cybersecurity . . . . . . . . . . . . 25

   8.1. The Double-Edged Sword of AI . . . . . . . . . . . . . . . . . . . . . . . 25

   8.2. Increasing Sophistication of Cyberattacks . . . . . . . . . . . . . . 25

   8.3. AI Algorithms Are Vulnerable to Attacks . . . . . . . . . . . . . . . 26

   8.4. Exploitation of Privacy and Personal Data . . . . . . . . . . . . . . 26

   8.5. Use of AI in Propagation of Deepfakes . . . . . . . . . . . . . . . . . 27

   8.6. Enablement of Autonomous Cyber Weapons . . . . . . . . . . . . 27

   8.7. Ensuring Robust AI Security . . . . . . . . . . . . . . . . . . . . . . . . . 27

9. Case Studies: AI and Cyberattack Scenarios . . . . . . . . . . . . . . . 29

   9.1. The Twitter Bitcoin Scam . . . . . . . . . . . . . . . . . . . . . . . . . . . . 29

   9.2. The Cloud Hopper Operation . . . . . . . . . . . . . . . . . . . . . . . . . 29

   9.3. The DarkTrace Case . . . . . . . . . . . . . . . . . . . . . . . . . . . . . . . . 30

   9.4. The DeepLocker Case . . . . . . . . . . . . . . . . . . . . . . . . . . . . . . . 30

   9.5. AI Deepfake Attacks . . . . . . . . . . . . . . . . . . . . . . . . . . . . . . . . 31

10. Future of Cybersecurity with AI: Opportunities and Challenges . 33

   10.1. Advent of AI in Cybersecurity . . . . . . . . . . . . . . . . . . . . . . . 33

   10.2. Opportunities Leveraged by AI . . . . . . . . . . . . . . . . . . . . . . . 34

      10.2.1. AI-empowered Defense . . . . . . . . . . . . . . . . . . . . . . . . 34

      10.2.2. Automation of Cybersecurity Tasks . . . . . . . . . . . . . . 34

      10.2.3. Predictive Analysis . . . . . . . . . . . . . . . . . . . . . . . . . . . 34

   10.3. Challenges Posed by AI . . . . . . . . . . . . . . . . . . . . . . . . . . . . . 35

10.3.1. AI-powered Cyberattacks . . . . . . . . . . . . . . . . . . . . . . . . . . . . 35

10.3.2. Data Privacy . . . . . . . . . . . . . . . . . . . . . . . . . . . . . . . . . . . 35

10.3.3. AI Bias . . . . . . . . . . . . . . . . . . . . . . . . . . . . . . . . . . . . . . . 35

10.4. Preparing for the Future . . . . . . . . . . . . . . . . . . . . . . . . . . . . . 35

10.4.1. Holistic approach to Cybersecurity . . . . . . . . . . . . . . . . . . 36

10.4.2. Collaboration between AI and Cybersecurity Experts . . 36

10.4.3. Legal and Ethical Frameworks . . . . . . . . . . . . . . . . . . . . . 36

11. Practical Steps to Enhance Cybersecurity in the Age of AI . . . . . . 38

11.1. Understanding Current Cybersecurity Risks . . . . . . . . . . . . 38

11.2. Developing a Robust Cybersecurity Framework . . . . . . . . . . 39

11.3. Applying AI in Cybersecurity Framework . . . . . . . . . . . . . . . 39

11.4. Training and Education . . . . . . . . . . . . . . . . . . . . . . . . . . . . . 40

11.5. Designing for Security . . . . . . . . . . . . . . . . . . . . . . . . . . . . . . 40

11.6. Collaborating for a Secure Future . . . . . . . . . . . . . . . . . . . . . 41

# Chapter 1. Introduction

In an age where digital landscapes continue to evolve at an unprecedented pace, the emergence of Artificial Intelligence (AI) adds a new layer of complexity to the existing cybersecurity paradigm. As a society increasingly intertwined with the digital realm, understanding the implications of these technologies and their intersections is paramount for our security. 'Cybersecurity in the Age of AI: Staying Safe in the Digital World' serves as your pragmatic guide to navigate this entangled web of concepts. With a step-by-step approach, we distill down highly technical details into readily digestible pieces. Regardless of your background or experience, this Special Report aims to equip you with the knowledge and actionable strategies needed to maintain both your personal and corporate digital safety in this fast-evolving cybersecurity landscape. Dive in for a comprehensive exploration of the topic that is as enlightening as it is practical.

# Chapter 2. Understanding Cybersecurity Basics

Cybersecurity is the practice of protecting digital infrastructures, systems, networks, devices, and data from cyber threats. With a constant evolution in technology, understanding its basic principles becomes vital in order to foster a secure digital environment. The knowledge of cybersecurity basics helps individuals and businesses safeguard their sensitive information, secure transactions, integral systems and software from being exploited by cybercriminals.

## 2.1. What is Cybersecurity?

At its core, cybersecurity is designed to protect digital systems and data against unauthorized access, use, disclosure, disruption, modification, or destruction, which could lead to serious consequences like data theft, financial loss, and damage to the reputation of organizations. Cyberattacks are complex and malicious acts that exploit vulnerabilities in a computing system or network, resulting in great damage or loss.

There are multiple complex layers in a secure digital system, which can be broadly categorized into three key components:

1. People: The individuals who use, manage or secure the systems.
2. Processes: The policies and procedures that define how to manage and secure the digital environment.
3. Technology: The tools and devices implemented to protect against cyber threats.

By focusing on these three dimensions of cybersecurity, organizations and individuals can craft a cybersecurity strategy that balances protection with usability.

# 2.2. Understanding the Threat Landscape

Understanding the threat landscape is foundational to cybersecurity basics. Cyber threats continuously evolving, adding complexity to our digital lives. These threats could be drafted by cybercriminals, hacktivists or state-sponsored actors and can hugely impact businesses, governments, and individuals. They can come in different forms such as:

1. Viruses

2. Worms

3. Trojans

4. Spyware

5. Ransomware

6. Malware

7. Phishing

8. DDoS attacks

9. SQL injection attacks

10. Man-in-the-Middle attacks

All these cyber threats have varying degrees of impact and utilize different attack vectors to achieve their objectives. Understanding the definition, underlying mechanisms, as well as possible countermeasures against each type of these attacks is pivotal in securing digital environments.

# 2.3. Cybersecurity Principles

Adopting the right cybersecurity principles is vital for ensuring an organization's digital safety. A few fundamental principles that are widely recognized in cybersecurity are:

1. Principle of Least Privilege: This principle advises that an individual, program, or system should have the minimum levels of access – or permissions – necessary to perform their function. This reduces the risk associated with superfluous privileges, such as data leaks and misuse.

2. Defense in Depth Principle: This cybersecurity principle suggests using multiple layers of security in order to protect critical assets. The rationale behind defense in depth is that if one layer of security fails, others still stand.

3. Principle of Integrity: It refers to maintaining the accuracy and consistency of data over its entire lifecycle. Measures must be taken to prevent unauthorized alteration of data.

4. Principle of Confidentiality: It is about protecting information from being disclosed to unauthorized parties.

5. Principle of Availability: It assures that system resources are available to authorized users when they need them.

These principles serve as a foundation in the cybersecurity domain for developing robust security policies and making informed decisions about secure systems design.

# 2.4. Cybersecurity Technologies and Best Practices

Understanding security technologies and their optimal use forms a pivotal part of the cybersecurity basics. While establishing an organisational cybersecurity strategy, it is essential to incorporate firewalls, antivirus software, encryption, intrusion detection systems, and other preventive measures.

Cyber Hygiene practices also play a major role in the security ecosystem. Regular patching of systems, secure password practices, multi-factor authentication, backing up data, limiting user access rights, and providing security training can go a long way in mitigating cyber threats.

With the growing prominence of Artificial Intelligence in cybersecurity, it's vital to understand how AI and machine learning can enable automated threat detection, behavioural analytics, incident response and inject scalability into the cybersecurity practice.

# 2.5. Legal and Ethical Considerations

As digital spaces continue to grow, so do the legal and ethical concerns surrounding cybersecurity. Regular debates occur worldwide on topics such as privacy rights, data ownership, surveillance, and cyber warfare. Therefore, keeping abreast with the legislative, regulatory, and ethical landscape in cybersecurity is an essential part of cybersecurity basics.

Cybersecurity awareness and preparedness are key to safeguarding any digital system. A comprehensive understanding of the foundation and evolving trends in cybersecurity will provide you with valuable insights into the pressing need for security in today's interconnected globe. The upcoming chapters are designed to delve deeper into the intricacies of each topic introduced in this chapter to provide a more in-depth understanding of staying safe in the digital world.

# Chapter 3. Unravelling the Concept of Artificial Intelligence

Artificial Intelligence, often abbreviated as AI, is a term that dates back to the mid-twentieth century, yet it continually bustles with a sense of novelty, promise, and at times, vague apprehension. To comprehend AI's role within our digital universe and explore how it elevates the gravity of cybersecurity, we must first unfurl its intricate threads.

## 3.1. Understanding the Basics

Artificial Intelligence, by definition, encapsulates computer systems designed to mimic human intelligence — 'intelligence' being the operative word. The human intellect can interpret complex data, learn from experience, execute tasks, adapt to fresh inputs, anticipate outcomes, and apply reason. AI systems are developed with the goal of replicating these abilities.

Two main AI strands surface in most discussions, each with separate but overlapping functionality: narrow (weak) AI, and general (strong) AI. Narrow AI (or weak AI) systems are constructed for specific tasks, such as voice recognition. These systems operate under limited predefined contexts and cannot reason beyond them.

General AI (or strong AI), on the other hand, possesses cognitive functionalities at par with human beings. It can understand, recognize, learn, and apply knowledge as humans do. However, despite the conceptual existence of General AI, it is still largely an uncontested theoretical frontier in the AI domain.

# 3.2. AI Methods: How Is Artificial Intelligence Achieved?

Artificial Intelligence functions primarily through machine learning (ML), and its subsequent evolution, deep learning (DL). But before we delve into these technical aspects, let's consider an example.

Imagine owning a smart thermostat that learns from your behavior. Over time, it adjusts the temperature settings based on patterns it has observed: you prefer a snug 22C when you are about to retire for the night, or you need a bright and balmy 25C to kickstart your mornings. This is AI at work, making your thermostat not just programmable but intuitively "smart."

A machine learning model is built on the foundation of this 'learning from experience'. Algorithms parse through data, learn from these data inputs, and make informed decisions or predictions, all while fine-tuning performance with each interaction.

Deep learning takes this a notch higher. It uses neural networks with several layers (hence, 'deep') for more complex data interpretation. To revert to our smart thermostat example, deep learning would allow the thermostat to consider additional data like weather forecasts or your electricity usage patterns, thereby enabling more nuanced temperature controls.

Whenever AI makes a prediction or decision, like determining email spam or recommending a movie, machine learning, and deep learning are at the helm. Alongside these, other AI techniques such as Natural Language Processing (NLP) and robotics are also used to simulate and replicate human-like actions and behaviors.

## 3.3. The Evolution of Artificial Intelligence

The inception of AI took place around the mid-20th century. Researchers hypothesized that machines could be programed to replicate human decision-making. The following years marked the development of the first AI systems, triggering a swell of expectations around their potential.

Unfortunately, the early AI touted as the harbinger of a new future soon bumped into technological limitations. Progress was slow and inconsistent until the advent of faster, more potent computers in the late 1990s. The burgeoning internet era generated sizeable data amounts, allowing machine learning algorithms to evolve and continually improve themselves.

The following decade ushered in the groundbreaking concept of 'deep learning,' a specialized machine learning subset, illuminating avenues for sophisticated AI application across diverse realms, from cybersecurity to healthcare.

## 3.4. AI in Our Lives Today

Today, AI's infusion in our lives is pervasive and silent. Voice assistants like Siri and Alexa, recommendations on your Netflix account, route suggestions on Google Maps, and face detection in your photo apps, are manifestations of AI. Additionally, AI's footprint in more vital and sensitive sectors like banking, healthcare, and defense amplify its impact and significance.

In sum, Artificial Intelligence, propelling our lives' conveniences, conveniences, and necessities, engineered to replicate human-like learning and decision-making, is far more than computer programming. As we continue to integrate this powerful tool into our digital structures and systems, the need to protect, control, and predict its actions and repercussions comes to the fore. It is this intersection of AI and cybersecurity we will explore in the subsequent chapters.

# Chapter 4. The Intersection of AI and Cybersecurity

The integration of Artificial Intelligence (AI) into cybersecurity has significantly altered the landscape, leading to new opportunities and challenges. It's a complex relationship worth understanding from a multidimensional perspective for a greater appreciation of the current state and future trajectories of cybersecurity.

## 4.1. The New Cybersecurity Battlefield

Advent of AI has converted cybersecurity into a brand new battlefield where both cyber offenders and defenders are rapidly leveraging AI to outperform each other. AI is being used to safeguard data, anticipate threats, and provide a more robust protective infrastructure. On the contrary, sophisticated AI tools provide powerful means for cybercriminals to orchestrate advanced cyber attacks. AI becomes a double-edged sword, simultaneously the defense and weapon of choice in the escalating cybersecurity arms race.

## 4.2. Leveraging AI for Cyber Defense

AI promises a multitude of benefits for cybersecurity. As the digital world expands, traditional human-based cybersecurity measures are finding it hard to cope up with the scale and complexity of threats.

Machine Learning (ML), a subset of AI, leverages pattern recognition to "learn" from vast amounts of data. Based on this learning, it can identify and react to threats and irregularities even in massive data sets. This ability is especially beneficial against zero-day attacks, where traditional methods fall short due to the lack of a priori knowledge.

AI and ML also alleviate the problem of false positives, enhancing the accuracy of threat detection. By learning what a regular network activity looks like, anomalies can be efficiently spotted, significantly reducing the rate of false alarms. The integration of AI in Intrusion Detection Systems (IDS) and intrusion prevention systems (IPS) provides real-time detection capabilities, continuously monitoring network traffic to identify and mitigate potential threats.

Additionally, AI enhances the analytic capabilities of Security Information and Event Management (SIEM) systems, gathering and analyzing security data across various networks, devices, and applications. AI-powered SIEM can facilitate rapid and precise threat detection and response to strengthen an organization's cybersecurity posture effectively.

# 4.3. AI as an Offensive Tool

While AI serves as a steadfast protector of cybersecurity, it, unfortunately, empowers cybercriminals with technological advancements for launching sophisticated attacks. AI can automate the process of finding network vulnerabilities and devise effective strategies to exploit them.

AI-powered malware is a horrifying reality. Such malware can adapt and learn from the defenses it comes across, modifying its tactics to infiltrate more effectively in the subsequent attacks. Furthermore, AI-driven phishing attacks can convincingly mimic human behavior to design personalized, persuasive, and targeted phishing campaigns.

AI also facilitates deepfakes and disinformation campaigns that can be catastrophic for individuals and organizations. By manipulating audio and video content, cybercriminals may stage fraudulent scenarios or instigate malicious propaganda, challenging the integrity and authenticity of digital content.

# 4.4. Preparing for an AI-Augmented Cyber Future

Amid the burgeoning arms race, organizations and individuals must evolve their cybersecurity strategies. AI and human experts will need to collaborate to effectively counter the mounting threat. Education and awareness about AI-driven threats are crucial to prevent falling prey to smart cyber-attacks.

Advanced AI-driven cybersecurity solutions must be adopted to provide effective defenses. Due to AI's inherent complexity, these solutions should be user-friendly and interpretable, offering insights into their working process, decisions, and actions.

Organizations should also encourage an AI-driven security culture, which prioritizes continuous learning, proactive threat detection, and rapid response. This would necessitate training programs and workshops to upskill employees in AI technologies and their cybersecurity functions.

In conclusion, the interception of AI and cybersecurity is a complex and evolving domain. While AI brings a host of opportunities, we must caution against the threats it creates. The constant development of adaptive AI-driven defenses, comprehensive understanding of AI's implications in cybersecurity, and fostering an AI-driven defense culture are crucial to ensuring safety against impending cyber threats in this digital age.

# Chapter 5. Threat Landscape in the AI Era

For many, the concept of artificial intelligence may elicit images of futuristic societies inhabited by functionally independent machines. However, the truth is that AI permeates our daily lives in much subtler yet significant ways, which makes it equally vulnerable to cyber threats.

Navigating in this rapidly evolving digital sea, the characteristics of the new threat landscape must be fully understood. Just as the industrial age saw a redefinition of warfare, the digital age filled with AI has restructured the battleground that is cybersecurity.

## 5.1. AI: Breeding Ground for Advanced Cyber Threats

As artificial intelligence becomes more commonplace, it also becomes a fresh target for malicious entities. AI systems are a potential gold mine for cybercriminals because they often contain large amounts of high-value data. Moreover, offences against an AI system can be difficult to detect and prove.

In addition to the traditional denial-of-service (DoS) threats, AI systems can be targeted in novel ways. In a method known as "Adversarial AI," the system is tampered with to produce incorrect results or behaviors. An example of this is the slight modification of an image pixel that results in an AI mistaking a pedestrian for a stop sign - a potentially deadly mistake in the context of autonomous vehicles.

This advanced threat landscape is becoming commonplace and is increasing in sophistication at an alarming rate. Therefore, understanding these new types of threats and developing meeting strategies to counter them is one of the prime priorities of cybersecurity experts.

## 5.2. AI Techniques as Cyber Threat Tools

Most alarmingly, AI can be used by attackers themselves to execute even more advanced attacks. Machine learning models can be trained to recognize patterns in a system's defenses and exploit them, or even automate phishing emails in unprecedented scale and sophistication.

Malicious uses of AI include the potential to automate tasks that would typically require human intelligence, such as targeted, "spear-phishing" attacks. Here, AI can automate the collection and analysis of personal information for creating highly effective attack vectors. This will make detection and prevention of such attacks significantly harder.

The growth of AI also poses the risk of automated hacking. Machine learning algorithms can be used by attackers to understand patterns, find vulnerabilities in software, and identify the optimum methods to exploit them. This use of AI could potentially lead to an increase in the speed and efficiency of cyber attacks, leaving little time for detection or response.

## 5.3. How AI Changes the Threat Environment

Another important aspect to consider is the decentralization of threats. With machine learning models becoming more accessible, not only corporations and state actors have the capabilities to run profound cyber attacks. Small groups or even individuals can also carry out sophisticated operations, using AI toolkits and off-the-shelf tools.

As AI proliferates, an increase in the diversity of threats has been observed, deploying strategies far advanced and more complex compared to previous eras. The cybersecurity landscape is transforming from simple, direct attacks to highly advanced undetected threats that are persistent and blend with typical network traffic.

Also, threats are moving from being reactive to being anticipatory due to the nature of AI, making cybersecurity a more complex game of offence and defence.

# 5.4. Mitigating the Threats of AI

While the threat landscape is evolving to become more challenging, AI also offers opportunities for improving cybersecurity. Behaviour analytics powered by AI can observe and detect abnormal actions, potentially blocking threats before they affect the system.

AI can assist in automating investigations into alerts, freeing cybersecurity personnel to focus on more critical tasks. More advanced security systems are beginning to rely on AI for detecting unusual patterns or anomalies in large amounts of data, offering potentials for more efficient and powerful security measures.

To successfully mitigate the newly emerging AI threats, organizations must adopt 'security by design' principles, incorporating threat intelligence and risk management into their AI systems right from the designing stage. While it's impossible to predict every possible vulnerability, working with the mindset of being 'secure by default' harnesses good practices that minimize security exploits.

In conclusion, AI holds a double-edged attribute in the cybersecurity space, offering both formidable challenges and promising capabilities. The induction of AI calls for considerable adjustments to our strategies, tools, and perceptions to safeguard cybersecurity in a landscape experiencing constant change. Whether the significant advances of AI will be a blessing or a curse to our cybersecurity infrastructure ultimately depends on our capability to adapt, evolve, and innovate.

# Chapter 6. AI-Driven Cybersecurity Solutions

Artificial Intelligence (AI) is rapidly infiltrating the cybersecurity domain, essentially reforming traditional defensive mechanisms with AI-driven solutions that are capable of predicting, mitigating, and swiftly responding to cyber threats. By leveraging AI, organizations can harness its immense computational power and custom learning capabilities, fortifying their cybersecurity infrastructures against increasingly sophisticated attacks.

## 6.1. The AI-Cybersecurity Integration

Utilizing AI for cybersecurity isn't an entirely novel concept; the cybersecurity industry has been toiling to embed AI into its frameworks, recognizing AI's potential in predicting and preventing cyber-attacks long before they occur. Machine Learning (ML), a branch of AI, has been instrumental in this integration.

ML enhances system capabilities to learn and improve from experience. It analyzes historical data, spots patterns, and makes future predictions, which can be applied in detecting abnormal behaviors or anomalies that may indicate a cybersecurity threat. This proactive functionality goes far beyond the capabilities of traditional security measures, which typically only react to threats once they've transpired.

## 6.2. Behavioral Analysis and Anomaly Detection

One of AI's significant contributions is the way it facilitates behavioral analysis to pinpoint anomalies. Traditionally, cybersecurity systems monitor network traffic and flag patterns that match known attack signatures. However, the downfall of such a method is its inability to detect zero-day attacks - threats that exploit software vulnerabilities unknown to those interested in patching them. It's in this context that AI shines.

AI-driven systems are constantly learning, improving their detection capabilities, and adapting to evolving threats. They understand patterns and can promptly find variations, marking them as anomalies. This continuous process of learning and refining allows AI to recognize emerging threats and unknown attack vectors, enabling quicker response times and more robust security measures.

## 6.3. AI in Action: Pattern Recognition

A core part of cybersecurity involves identifying patterns, a task AI excels at. ML algorithms can sift through millions of data points, automatically detecting patterns that could represent an attack. And deep learning, a more complex subset of ML, can even predict attackers' next moves based on their modus operandi, immediately responding and preventing potential breaches.

Unfortunately, this pattern recognition skill is a double-edged sword. While it helps protect an organization, it can also be exploited by ill-intentioned actors who can deploy AI to find vulnerabilities in a system.

## 6.4. AI-Powered Phishing Detection

Phishing is a prevalent method of cyberattacks where attackers impersonate a trusted entity to trick individuals into revealing sensitive information. Traditional Anti-Phishing tools typically rely on blacklists and rule-based systems, struggling with evolving phishing techniques and zero-day phishing URLs.

AI can significantly improve phishing detection. By analyzing an extensive and diverse array of features from email content to URL patterns, AI can build robust models. These models can not only discern between legitimate and phishing web pages but also adapt to evolving styles of phishing attacks.

# 6.5. Enhancing Incident Response With AI

A necessary function in a cybersecurity program is incident response, aimed at minimizing the impact of a breach. Traditional incident response often involves time-consuming procedures and relies heavily on human intervention.

AI can revolutionize this process in several ways. It can automate routine tasks, flag significant incidents that require human intervention, and even suggest the most effective countermeasures based on previous similar events. AI can contribute significantly to the speed and efficiency of an organization's response, limiting potential damage.

Despite these advancements, AI is not a cure-all for cybersecurity challenges. Increasing reliance on AI may spur new types of cyber threats. As AI models become more complex, they might become black boxes, making it nearly impossible to understand their decision-making process or predict their actions when they encounter unseen threats. Critics also highlight the risks associated with adversarial AI, where attackers use AI to identify vulnerabilities or launch sophisticated attacks.

As we move into an era of increasingly AI-driven cybersecurity solutions, it's important that we focus on developing resilient AI systems. These need to be robust enough to withstand attacks, interpretable enough to understand and oversee, and agile enough to adapt to ever-evolving cyber threats. While the journey ahead seems challenging, the promising potential of AI in cybersecurity is undeniable. By harnessing this potential effectively and responsibly, we can look forward to a stronger defense against the cyber threats of tomorrow.

# Chapter 7. Role and Impact of Machine Learning in Cybersecurity

As an emergent field bridging data-driven algorithms and cybersecurity, machine learning presents an array of opportunities and challenges. This chapter offers an in-depth exploration of the role and impact of machine learning in cybersecurity—the impetus, mechanisms, and implications.

This chapter will build on a core understanding without losing sight of the practical applications of these complex concepts. It will elucidate the role of machine learning and dive deep into various facets: infrastructure security, fraud detection, malware detection, privacy, and potential adversarial attacks on the ML models themselves.

## 7.1. The Intersection of Machine Learning and Cybersecurity

Beginning at the intersection of these two evolving fields, we must first understand that machine learning is simply a tool and should be regarded as thus. It's a computational method for enhancing or automating decision-making processes by utilizing statistical models—trained on vast swathes of data—to understand patterns and make predictions.

The cybersecurity landscape, on the other hand, is one of constant dynamism, filled with evolving threats and vulnerabilities. The sheer volume of threats, and their frequent evolution, makes it nearly impossible for traditional cyber defense methods to keep pace. This is where machine learning steps in, deploying its predictive abilities to identify threats and protect vulnerable systems before they could be exploited.

# 7.2. Infrastructure Security and Machine Learning

The fundamental bedrock of any digital system is its underlying infrastructure, the security of which is a primary concern. Machine learning algorithms can ensure this security by investigating abnormal network traffic, identifying strange patterns, and predicting possible attack vectors.

Machine learning models, trained on past network data and known anomalies, can effectively identify unusual occurrences. These algorithms can spot patterns reminiscent of DDoS attacks, intrusions, or other risks, alerting the security team proactively about potential vulnerabilities or ongoing attacks. The adaptive nature of machine learning makes these algorithms perpetually improve with more exposure to network traffic and threat data.

# 7.3. Fraud Detection

Fraud detection is another critical area where machine learning has proven its worth. Machine learning algorithms—particularly unsupervised learning methods like clustering or anomaly detection—are masterful at identifying and isolating abnormal behavior.

In the field of financial cybersecurity, these algorithms are deployed to identify suspicious transactions based on several factors: transaction value, region, time, frequency, and more. By comparing these transactions to typical trends, these algorithms can flag potential fraudulent activity, protecting organizations and users from breaches.

# 7.4. Identifying and Countering Malware

Machine learning has been a breakthrough development in the battle against malicious software. Traditional tools—reliant on signature-based detection—were combatting the proliferation of malware variants. Machine learning provides a more sophisticated approach.

Using techniques like Natural Language Processing (NLP), machine learning can dissect the code structure of software, identifying potential malicious patterns. By learning from pervasive malware signatures, ML models can identify and isolate new malware variants more effectively and efficiently than their conventional counterparts.

# 7.5. Privacy Concerns and Mechanisms

While machine learning serves as an excellent tool for cybersecurity, it also introduces unique privacy concerns. Machine Learning models need vast amounts of data for training, raising legitimate privacy concerns about the source and nature of this data.

Methods such as Differential Privacy offer a potential solution, allowing ML models to learn patterns without gaining access to specific personal details. This balance between effective machine learning and privacy protection is a tricky but essential aspect to address.

# 7.6. Adversarial Attacks on Machine Learning Models

While machine learning is a powerful tool for cybersecurity, it can also be a target. Adversarial attacks use input data to manipulate ML model outcomes—often without detection. These cyber threats can severely impact ML-based cybersecurity systems.

# 7.7. Moving Forward: Ensuring the Safe Use of Machine Learning in Cybersecurity

Machine learning's role in cybersecurity will continue to expand as the digital landscape evolves. It is incumbent upon us, as cybersecurity professionals and digital citizens, to understand and modulate its use—balancing its potential with its challenges.

With due diligence in data privacy, resilience against adversarial attacks, and continuously adapting to the fluctuating cyber threatscape, ML-powered cybersecurity can lead to safer digital environments. Thereby, stakeholder understanding and participation is integral to secure the digital frontier in this age of AI.

To conclude, machine learning indeed has its challenges in cybersecurity, but the potential benefits far surpass the hurdles. With better understanding and a proactive approach, the aim should be to harness ML's power for robust and resilient cybersecurity infrastructure.

# Chapter 8. Risks and Vulnerabilities of AI in Cybersecurity

Artificial Intelligence (AI) promises to revolutionize numerous industries, including cybersecurity, but its adoption also presents a host of new vulnerabilities and risks. Recognizing these vulnerabilities allows us to develop safeguards and strategies to continue leveraging AI securely.

## 8.1. The Double-Edged Sword of AI

AI is a double-edged sword in cybersecurity. On one side, it can reinforce defenses and aid in identifying threats faster and with greater accuracy. However, in the wrong hands, AI can also give cybercriminals new tools to launch more sophisticated attacks.

Cybercriminals can exploit AI in various ways such as automating their attacks, utilizing AI systems to analyze large quantities of data for vulnerabilities, or employing it to disguise their activities. There is a growing concern that as AI becomes more advanced, it will become more accessible to cybercriminals.

## 8.2. Increasing Sophistication of Cyberattacks

AI has enabled cyberattacks to become more sophisticated and robust than conventional hacking methods. For example, AI can now generate phishing emails that seem genuine to the extent where it fools both humans and security systems. Cybercriminals can thus exploit AI through spear phishing. They can train systems to imitate executives' writing styles, tricking recipients into sharing sensitive information.

Moreover, AI can also facilitate advanced persistent threats (APTs) which stealthily and continuously target a specific entity. AIs can learn and help the APT evolve to avoid detection and continue to infiltrate the system.

# 8.3. AI Algorithms Are Vulnerable to Attacks

AI algorithms and systems aren't infallible and are susceptible to attacks. Data poisoning, one such attack on AI systems, involves the manipulation of training data to influence the behavior of the AI system. This can result in compromised network traffic analysis, causing the AI to classify harmful traffic as safe.

Moreover, adversarial attacks present another significant vulnerability. They involve manipulating an AI's input data to fool the system, causing it to misinterpret data and make incorrect decisions. This can severely compromise an AI-based cybersecurity system and may allow harmful traffic to pass undetected.

# 8.4. Exploitation of Privacy and Personal Data

As AI systems generally require vast amounts of data to function correctly, there's an inherent risk that this data could be misused by cybercriminals. These systems can store personal, financial and business-critical data, providing a potential goldmine for criminals. Furthermore, AI, particularly machine learning algorithms, often functions as a 'black box,' making misuse of data even harder to detect.

## 8.5. Use of AI in Propagation of Deepfakes

One of the more troubling uses of AI in cybercrime is the creation of deepfakes. Deepfakes involve manipulating images, videos, or audio to depict scenes or speech that did not actually occur, and can be used to propagate misinformation, deceive individuals or systems, and even impersonate executives or high-ranking officials.

## 8.6. Enablement of Autonomous Cyber Weapons

AI can also pave the way for the creation of autonomous cyber weapons. An autonomous cyber weapon uses AI to make decisions about targets, timing, and execution methods. These weapons can perform cyberattacks with little to no human intervention, potentially resulting in more widespread and severe attacks.

## 8.7. Ensuring Robust AI Security

Despite these risks and vulnerabilities, adopting AI is clearly beneficial if done thoughtfully and securely. To ensure robust AI security, organizations should follow best practices, including performing thorough risk assessments, actively monitoring AI systems, and maintaining data privacy. Additionally, the human element in AI security should not be overlooked. Staff should be trained to understand AI vulnerabilities and how to spot and respond to potential issues.

In conclusion, the use of AI in cybersecurity brings about new vulnerabilities and risks. As the technology advances and becomes more commonplace, organizations need to recognise these potential threats and take measures to reduce their impact. By doing so, the benefits of AI in cybersecurity can be greatly unleashed.

From increasing the sophistication of attacks and exploiting privacy issues, to being vulnerable to adversarial and data poisoning attacks, AI's capabilities can be harnessed by cybercriminals for malicious purposes. Security best practices need to be incorporated and continuous vigilance maintained to ensure AI enhances security as it is intended to, rather than providing new avenues for cyber threats.

# Chapter 9. Case Studies: AI and Cyberattack Scenarios

In the modern digital landscape, AI has surfaced as a dual-edge sword, facilitating both the ploys of cyber attackers and the robustness of defense systems. To understand the full scope of AI's implications in cybersecurity, here are some case studies discussing well-known AI and cyberattack scenarios.

## 9.1. The Twitter Bitcoin Scam

In July 2020, Twitter was rocked by a monumental hack which saw attackers gain access to high-profile accounts such as Bill Gates, Elon Musk, Barack Obama, and other established entities. The perpetrators leveraged these compromised accounts to propagate a cryptocurrency scam, promising to double the Bitcoin sent to a certain address.

The ingenious facet of this attack was the use of AI to rapidly test and adjust their approach, tweaking variables such as the Bitcoin address and the text of the tweet until they found the most effective strategy. This exploit was worth a reported $118,000 in Bitcoin. AI enabled efficiency and adaptation at a pace unreached by human hackers previously, thus magnifying the effectiveness and speed of the attack.

## 9.2. The Cloud Hopper Operation

In this instance, cyber attackers, allegedly backed by the Chinese government, targeted Managed IT Service Providers (MSPs) to indirectly reach their clients. This attack, also known as the Cloud Hopper operation, was distinguished for its prolonged, stealthy nature.

Reportedly, the attackers used an AI-based botnet to automate and upscale the entire operation. The artificially intelligent network of interconnected bots sniffed out vulnerabilities, autonomously replicated themselves, and penetrated systems on an industrial scale. AI's capacity to perform advanced tasks endlessly without fatigue empowered this relentless, invasive attack.

## 9.3. The DarkTrace Case

Emerging as a beacon of AI's potential in cybersecurity, DarkTrace serves as an ideal case study of AI-powered defense systems. The firm's cyber 'immune system' illustrates AI's positive role in democratizing effective cybersecurity solutions.

Darktrace's model is premised on machine learning and AI to identify, understand, and combat threats in networks in real-time, without any significant human intervention. The system learns 'normal' behavior from undoubtedly safe actions and uses the deviations from this learned behavior to pinpoint cyber threats. Darktrace's approach, contrasting the rule-based system, is particularly potent against novel, unanticipated threats.

## 9.4. The DeepLocker Case

Discovered by IBM Research, DeepLocker is a new class of highly evasive and targeted malware. What sets DeepLocker apart is its blending of AI, specifically, neural networks, and encryption methods. As a result, it could hide its true intentions until it reached its specific target, appearing harmless and remaining undetected by traditional security systems.

To designate its target, DeepLocker could take an array of discriminants into account, such as facial recognition information, geolocation, or even voice recognition. Once the designated target is met, the malicious payload is triggered. AI's advanced processing ability made DeepLocker stealthy, targeted, and devastatingly effective.

# 9.5. AI Deepfake Attacks

Deepfake technology, though potentially having benign uses, is perhaps most recognized for its misuse, notably in generating counterfeit videos for crimes such as identity theft, fraud, and misinformation. Deepfakes are created by using AI to map one person's face onto another in a video. The degree of realism can be so high that distinguishing deepfakes from real data is increasingly challenging.

As an instance, in 2019, a UK-based energy firm's CEO was mimicked via AI algorithms to execute a voice deepfake attack. The impersonator on the phone directed the company's executive to transfer €220,000 to a supplier with the assurance of reimbursement. However, the return of funds never happened, and the firm fell victim to one of the first publicly reported deepfake fraud cases.

These case studies exemplify how AI has indubitably transformed the cybersecurity landscape. An understanding of these incidents offers crucial insights into the nature of this evolving threat and, subsequently, enlightens us on our path to devise better, more robust countering strategies. AI is an overpowering tool, and in whose hands it rests may decide the trajectory of future digital safety. This ever-evolving domain of cybersecurity necessitates continuous learning, diligence, and adaptability to stay safe in the digital world.

In conclusion, AI's influence on cybersecurity is indisputable, seeing its application both in breaching protective measures and strengthening them. AI's capacity to simplify complex tasks, learn patterns, and adapt expeditiously testifies to its vast potential. However, our capability to wield this technology prudently and ethically will determine its impact on our digital security in the future. This tug-of-war between illicit and protective uses of AI will define the future of cybersecurity. It is vital to recognize the dual nature of AI to secure our digital universe effectively. The expanding possibilities underpin the urgency to equip society with the necessary knowledge and tools to navigate this intricate landscape safely.

# Chapter 10. Future of Cybersecurity with AI: Opportunities and Challenges

The technosphere has consistently welcomed revolutionary capabilities inspired by the burgeoning field of Artificial Intelligence (AI). Its abilities propose a future where structures become self-sufficient, our interactions seamless, and processes automated. However, along with these prospects, AI presents unique challenges in the realm of cybersecurity that mandates the reassessment of our current security infrastructures. In a world intertwined with a digital matrix, we must question, adapt, and reassess our standing on data security at regular intervals.

## 10.1. Advent of AI in Cybersecurity

In essence, AI refers to the simulation of human intelligence processes, inclusive of learning, reasoning, and self-correction, into machines. Incorporation of AI in cybersecurity means the evolution of defense mechanisms that can identify threats proactively, automate responses, and adapt to the rapidly changing cyber crime landscape.

AI and Machine Learning (ML) have been instrumental in predicting and neutralizing threats preemptively. Extended applications of AI and ML in cybersecurity include anomaly detection, recognizing patterns across vast databanks of log files or network flow data, automating responses to incidents, and predicting attacks based on perceived threat landscapes.

# 10.2. Opportunities Leveraged by AI

Considering the benefits AI brings to the table, traditional rule-based security measures become redundant. AI-powered security implies transitioning from a reactive security model to a proactive one, where threats are identified before they mutate into an attack.

## 10.2.1. AI-empowered Defense

AI's adaptive, machine learning capabilities offer a significant contribution to building superior defensive strategies. For instance, AI can identify patterns across large datasets, pinpointing anomalies, and providing real-time alerts on potential threats. This proactive defense mechanism minimally disrupts the workflow and reduces downtime.

## 10.2.2. Automation of Cybersecurity Tasks

Routine tasks such as risk assessment, monitoring, incident responses can be automated, freeing up the human workforce's bandwidth. Moreover, AI algorithms are capable of performing tasks at an unmatched speed and efficiency, thereby enhancing the overall operational efficiency of cybersecurity teams.

## 10.2.3. Predictive Analysis

One of the significant advantages of AI is its ability to provide predictive analysis. Considering historical patterns, tactics, and recorded attacks, AI can predict possible risk areas that could be hit in the future, enabling the preemptive implementation of security measures.

## 10.3. Challenges Posed by AI

While AI does promise zephyrs of change in a positive direction, it also introduces unique challenges that the cybersecurity world must be prepared to meet.

### 10.3.1. AI-powered Cyberattacks

Contrary to popular belief, AI isn't exclusive to defense mechanisms. As an open-source technology, equivalent, if not more dangerous, AI algorithms can be employed by malicious entities to launch more sophisticated, hard-to-detect cyberattacks. Thus, the advancement of AI and ML necessitates the advancement of defense.

### 10.3.2. Data Privacy

AI's functioning is fundamentally dependent on vast amounts of data. However, data collection, storage, and access introduce a suite of concerns regarding user privacy. Manifestations of these concerns vary from regulators pushing for more stringent data regulations to consumers demanding better data handling practices.

### 10.3.3. AI Bias

AI systems, since their intelligence is based on the data that trains them, are prone to inherent human biases present in the data. These biases can result in flawed cybersecurity decisions and malicious exploitation by cybercriminals.

## 10.4. Preparing for the Future

An evolving landscape of AI-powered cybersecurity systems, complete with its array of opportunities and challenges, is inevitable. Several adjustments could be made today to ensure we're prepared better for tomorrow.

### 10.4.1. Holistic approach to Cybersecurity

We need to adopt a multi-pronged approach that involves everyone within an organization - from management to entry-level employees. Providing quality cybersecurity training to employees can significantly minimize human errors, which are often the weakest links in security chains.

### 10.4.2. Collaboration between AI and Cybersecurity Experts

The interdisciplinary nature of cybersecurity means architects and other relevant IT personnel must work closely with AI experts to build the best defense systems. This collaboration will be essential for early threat identification, remediation, and recovery.

### 10.4.3. Legal and Ethical Frameworks

To mitigate AI bias and data privacy issues, governments must establish a regulatory framework to ensure ethical and responsible AI use. Organizations must comply with these data privacy regulations and build transparency into their AI applications.

The emerging interplay between AI and cybersecurity is complex and evolving rapidly. It holds immense potential to transform cybersecurity as we know it, but equally has severe implications if mismanaged. To leverage the promises of the AI-driven future, one needs to brace for the challenges it entails and adapt with agility.

In essence, the future of cybersecurity with AI paints a picture that's simultaneously hopeful and challenging. It nudges us out of our comfort zones, pushing us towards a reality that has begun to take form. As we stand on this precipice, it's essential to understand that AI doesn't spell the end but rather a new dawn for cybersecurity.

The arena of cybersecurity, underlined with layers of AI, will continue to evolve. Through a dynamic interplay of vigilance, innovation, and risk-mitigation, we could potentially inhabit a future that embraces the digital domain's opportunities without the constant worry of catastrophes. The journey is difficult and laden with obstacles, but with resilience, we might finally venture into a world where digital safety isn't a privilege but a standard.

# Chapter 11. Practical Steps to Enhance Cybersecurity in the Age of AI

Your venture into strengthening cybersecurity begins with an understanding of the fundamental concepts. To ensure a strong cybersecurity infrastructure in the age of AI, we need to synthesize strategies from both realms. Coupled with a forward-thinking mentality, you can outpace potential cyber threats, ensuring a secure digital presence for you or your organization.

## 11.1. Understanding Current Cybersecurity Risks

In the digital age, cybersecurity risks take various forms such as malware, phishing, ransomware, and DDoS attacks. Each type of attack targets systems or users in different ways, thus necessitating different lines of defense. Understanding AI presents another tangential path that cyber threats exploit.

For instance, machine learning (ML), a subset of AI, is a powerful tool that can accelerate the detection and mitigation of cyber threats. However, ML algorithms can also become targets of cyber attackers. Such attacks can either sabotage the algorithm's functionality (adversarial attacks) or steal sensitive information (data poisoning). Hence, a thorough understanding of AI threats is essential for effective cybersecurity strategies.

## 11.2. Developing a Robust Cybersecurity Framework

Establishing a robust cybersecurity framework entails a mix of policies, tools, and practices designed to protect your systems. It revolves around five key pillars: Identify, Protect, Detect, Respond, and Recover.

**Identify:** You need to understand your digital assets, as well as the cyber threats relevant to your organization or personal situation.

**Protect:** Implement safeguards to ensure the delivery of critical services. This might include firewalls, encryption tools, multi-factor authentication, and regular software updates.

**Detect:** Establish and apply mechanisms to identify the occurrence of a cybersecurity event quickly.

**Respond:** Conduct analysis after a cybersecurity event is detected. Determine and implement actions to contain the impact, often involving a mix of isolation, mitigation, and communication.

**Recover:** Develop and implement strategies to restore capabilities that were impaired due to a cybersecurity event.

## 11.3. Applying AI in Cybersecurity Framework

While implementing a robust cybersecurity system, AI offers potent tools for the fight against cyber threats. Here's how AI impacts each aspect of the cybersecurity framework.

**Identify:** Advanced AI algorithms can map and identify vulnerabilities within your systems, predicting future attacks based on historical data and patterns.

**Protect:** AI can assist in optimizing encryption algorithms and advance your authentication processes, making your digital fortress more impervious to potential breaches.

**Detect:** AI's exceptional prowess in data analysis can lead to quicker detection of anomalies and threats. For instance, machine learning algorithms can identify malware patterns that a human observer might miss.

**Respond:** AI can not only help detect an attack but also automate the response, thereby reducing the time it takes to react and contain a threat.

**Recover:** AI can support recovery efforts by predicting optimal recovery routes, helping organizations return to normal operations more quickly.

# 11.4. Training and Education

Investing in ongoing cybersecurity education and training is critical. The nature of cyber threats evolves constantly, and regularly updated training is essential to stay ahead of the game. Organizations should conduct regular cybersecurity drills using AI-enabled simulation tools, while individuals should view education on cybersecurity as an ongoing process, not a one-off task.

# 11.5. Designing for Security

When building digital infrastructures, security should be built into each development cycle. This includes Following the principles of Secure by Design and Privacy by Design. Securing from the start can prevent costly and damaging breaches down the line. AI can be part of this process, for example through automated code reviews or by identifying potential security bottlenecks in system designs.

# 11.6. Collaborating for a Secure Future

A solitary approach to cybersecurity is no longer viable. Fostering collaboration – within organizations, between organizations, and across nations – will be a key driver of cybersecurity resilience in the AI age. Information sharing about new threats, vulnerabilities, or effective countermeasures can significantly enhance collective cybersecurity.

In conclusion, to navigate the complex panorama of AI and cybersecurity, a multifaceted and dynamic approach is crucial. Embracing AI doesn't simply mean adopting new technology; it also entails acknowledging and mitigating its associated risks, ensuring ample security in the digital age.